Precious Work

Poems as Signposts In Residential Dementia Care

Foreword by Eric Midwinter, OBE

ℰ

Vanessa Young

Inklemaker

This first edition published in 2021 by
Inklemaker
63B Buxton Road, Weymouth DT4 9PL
email: *inklemaker@aol.com*

ISBN 978-0-95-462717-1

Copyright © Vanessa Young

The right of Vanessa Young to be identified as
the author of this work has been asserted by her
in accordance with
The Copyright, Designs & Patents Act 1988

All rights reserved. No part of this publication may be
reproduced, transmitted, or stored in a retrieval
system, in any form or by any means (electronic,
mechanical, photocopying, recording or otherwise)
without the prior written consent of the copyright
owner and her publisher.

Printed in Great Britain by
Advantage Digital Print Limited,
Dorchester DT2 9FT

Dedication

To all front-line carers and medical staff, and
other specialist workers who use this unusual guide,
among whom are
community and social workers, architects,
gardeners, trainees, curriculum advisers,
health & safety officers, building consultants,
journalists, planners, podiatrists, receptionists,
dieticians, librarians, building designers,
lecturers, civil servants, shareholders,
Government inspectors, charity workers,
cleaners, cooks, legal representatives
and physiotherapists.

Also, to those whose voices are represented here,
including a new resident who was heard to say,

*'We don't know where we are, what we want,
or if we're getting it.'*

Contents

Foreword by Eric Midwinter, OBE   7

Preface   9

Section I - CHOOSING

Work Experience Assignment
conducted two metres apart
during Covid-19, 2020   13
Starting to Choose   14
Operatics   15
Tailor-made   16
Alpha Beta   17

Section II - LIFE INSIDE

Chair   21
No Mirror   22
Life Inside   23
Chatting   24
Sofa   25
Visit   26
Pill   27
Tea   28
Interiors   29
Rota   30
Agency   31
Experts: Permitted Covid-19 Care Home
Visit, July 2020   32
You said ... Care Home Meeting for
all staff and residents   33
Upstairs, Downstairs   34
Sorrow   35
Who said?   36

The Peach	37
Jigsaw	38
First Response	39
No Wool	40
Question	41

Section III - NO EXIT

Second Wife	45
Handbag	46
Mayday Call	47
Polite Request	48
Departure	49

Section IV - HOW IT ALL BEGAN

Message	53
Secateurs	54
Diagnosis Blues	56
Doctor's Review	57
Forecast Unsettled	58
Context	60

The Connection – About the Author 61

Acknowledgements 64

Purpose 65

Foreword

It is troubling that the approaches to the treatment of the dreaded curse of dementia often lack a positive and imaginative tack. They can be clinically and physically normative, whilst lacking a wholistic grasp of how to meet the challenge of a personality thus so badly affected. This is amplified when being dealt with in units specialising in dementia where sufferers have been obliged to leave home for good or ill and become part of a large contingent.

The poet Vanessa Young has chosen to use verse as a signpost towards addressing the question of what is good practice in care by taking the essence of what she has heard and seen the sufferers themselves, and others, express (when she was visiting her mother in various dementia care units and hospitals) and converting it into easy-to-read poems.

The purpose of this educationally valid and important pocket guide is to offer access and instant insight into the types and levels of distress these residents can suffer so that those involved in this precious work can more openly discuss and subscribe to the most helpful responses to care.

Eric Midwinter, OBE, 2021

Preface

This poetical guide has been designed for anybody connected in any way to residential homes that offer dementia care as a specialism. It is intended to contribute to each individual bringing a little of their own magic into this sad and difficult area. As may be deduced from some of the poems, the field of specialist workers whose impact may make that magic difference is broad indeed.

Nobody can be perfect in any situation but my aim is that a few of these poems may become working tools. If they are useful in discussion or problem-solving, if they clarify good practice, if they are beneficial in training or even research topics, then this book achieves its goal.

As poet, I can only say that it is the sufferers themselves of this arresting and, ultimately, totally-destructive disease who have provided the stimulus and content. I simply found myself present among them, which spurred me on to absorb what I needed to develop a long-standing concern. The not unusual reason I gained access to their company was that it fell to me to be my mother's imperfect companion from her early-onset dementia to her life's ending at ninety-nine and a half years. This experience led me inexorably into the world of dementia care in residential settings.

VY, 2021

SECTION I - CHOOSING

Work Experience Assignment
conducted two metres apart during Covid-19, 2020

Who are the people sitting here?

They are old people
now in care.
What did they do?
We're never told;
we only need to know
just where they are
and in which chair.

What would their interests be?

We don't know,
we're not required to;
a cup of tea might give a clue.
Take one over, and
see what you can do.
But as for what they did
and what they now
could do, who knows.

Do you find the work interesting?

Well, our job is to *care*.
Increasing numbers
keep us always on the run
and Covid's not much fun, but
give it a try, why don't you?
It's life and death for all of us
but we don't make a fuss!
I haven't seen you here before
so, when you leave,
please lock the door.

Starting to Choose

What a lovely house!

And garden in front.

They say that
inside
the staff take the brunt.

What's more
round the back
there's a
definite
lack.

Operatics
sung daily in the summer season

Manager
(Soprano
or Tenor)

Sung to visitors:

You'll never see the garden
empty.
Cushioned seats around
are plenty.
Down the paths admire the view.
So, come with me,
oh, come with me
and
I'll show you!

Members of Staff
(Mezzo-sopranos
Altos: Refrain)
Standing by the French windows:

Rare the days the staff are plenty
so, the garden's always empty.

Residents
(Chorus)

Seated inside:

The garden waits for us they say!
So peaceful and so empty.
Only two staff here today.
Would there would be plenty …
Oh, would there
would be
plenty!

Tailor-made

The brochure was so clear
for relatives and those held dear.
Unrivalled standards
Staff who care
so, bring
your best-beloved
here!

The patterned curtains
green and brown,
new chairs that match;
we'll show you round.
You'll never make
a better choice
for loved ones with no say
or voice.

Look at the garden
through the gate.
Contribute to our
Garden Fete!

A cup of tea?

What *were*
the dates you said?

We'll see if we can find
a bed.

Alpha beta

U is slipping fast away
Y has lost its wherefore
L is lost and gone away
ABC *D mentia*

The letter *T* is takes away
And *P* is just for pay
To hell with this old alphabet
Chuck the thing away.

SECTION II - LIFE INSIDE

Chair

This is my chair by the table
They put me here each day
I'd get up if I were able
But here is
where I
stay.

No Mirror

There are doors to be opened
and blinds to be drawn
whether teatime or daytime
or no time at all.
But if I cross the floor,
try to get up and go
the door will be closed and
someone says, 'No'.

So, we sit with our backs
to the way we came in
and no mirror reflects
the state we are in.

They tell me the wallpaper
shows the sea shore
and home for me now is a chair,
not much more.
And I'll tell you this
if you're coming in new:
you'll do nowt else but rest
as there's nowt else to do.

We sit with our backs
to the way we came in.
No mirror reflects
the state we are in.

Life Inside

There was a manager who cared.
You know, we were quite
unprepared!
She came –
I don't remember when –
and made each long day
fun again.

For six whole months
they let her stay, and then
they sent her on her way:
told her to take
a holiday.

You wouldn't know
as you've just come.
Your life inside has
just begun.

Chatting

I know what should be done
    and I'm nearly
   a hundred and one.

Oh, yes, I agree with you
    and I'm nearly
   a hundred and two.

Sofa

We talk of what we hope is true ...

'My husband's going to take me home!'

'My husband's calling me by phone!'

... we talk of how we spent our lives,
our men and how we were their wives,
the places, things we used to do, and
all about our mothers too!

'Children?
I would have liked a few
but what was there for me to do?
I was his second wife
and he'd already fathered two.'

'Children!
Oh, yes, we had four and
could have easily had some more
but I was busy with the war,
with lots of extra work
to do.'

'And I worked all the
whole war too!'

'Who are these other people here?
Not one of them do I hold dear.'

Visit

My husband
has wheeled in
a duck on a stick.
Can someone
tell him
what to do
with it?

Pill

I remember in the war
meeting Mother at the door!
And *I* remember having twins and
lots of other funny things!
I remember life in York,
and all we had to do at work!

We did all this, I'm telling you.
But now,
what's there for us to do?
And tell us
what is there to say
when we do *nothing* every day?

We're all in here
just sitting still.
From time to time
we take a pill.
But you know what?
I don't
feel
ill.

Tea

Too late for tea
that comes around
the patterned curtains
hanging down.

Too soon to bed,
the patterned curtains
green and red.

Interiors

That looming clock,
high on the wall
is not for us at all. They keep watch
who keep the carpets clean
behind my chair,
beside,
between.

For us
time matters
not a bit.
Perhaps there's
somewhere else to sit,
look through a window pane.

I'd like to see the living grass
that every year grows green,
yes …
that every year
grows green again.

Rota

Where are the staff
for us today?
I saw one go the other way.
And someone said, 'There's one away'.

There's much at stake if they're at break;
I'll not get there in time.

I saw one pass. They're here at last!
Is it your turn
or mine?

Agency

The clock runs fast
for those with work to do.
They sent me here just now.
I'm new.

What first?
Has anybody quenched
the sitters' thirst?

Here, on my own,
I cannot say.
And who can tell me
anyway?

Experts:
Permitted Covid-19 Care Home Visit
July 2020

So, *you're* going into *lockdown*!
Oh really, is that new?
We have been in lockdown
since it was
'the thing to do',
if you had the sort of memory
with small holes
going through
and
could not
remember
where you lived,
or what you used to do.
They put you into lockdown.
That's what they did
with you.

So, if *you're* going into lockdown
and think it could be new
you've come to see
the experts.
Lockdown
is what
we do!

You said …
Care Home Meeting
for all staff and residents

'We're moving out of here,
to some of you a home so dear.
This rambling place will be pulled down;
a new one built just out of town.
And so, we need to hold a meeting
(should be ample seating!)
to hear what *you*'d all like to say
and learn from you
what would be best to do.
The plans are on the drawing board.
We'd like the best we can afford!'

**

That's what *you* said!

But now it's done
I can't say it's much fun.
Where can you swing a cat
or anything like that?

Upstairs, downstairs

We're all in a room
 upstairs.
We can't get down;
 who cares?

Sorrow

There's a courtyard outside
where people
can sit.
If it's sunny and hot
it would not take a lot
to get us all down
to that
wonderful spot.

But inside we stay
growing less and less fit.
We don't know anyway.
That's the sorrow
of it.

Who said?

You said
that I was
in a fight;
that something
I said
wasn't right.
You speak
as though I'm
not too bright.
Please someone,
can you
shed
some light?

The Peach

In a bowl
there sits a juicy,
rosy peach
beside a jug
of cooling water
that I cannot
reach.

Jigsaw

You've given me a jigsaw
with a thousand bits to fill.
The picture isn't very clear;
each piece identical.
I've had it for six months now
or it could be a year.
You say that I should finish it,
here, sitting in my chair.

The picture is a clifftop,
the colours blue and green;
not the most inspiring picture
I have ever seen.

'Why don't you do your jigsaw?'
If you say that once more
it would be my greatest pleasure
to tip it on the floor.

First Response

The trolley rattles round
at night,
'*Hot drinks*' their Evensong.
Somehow,
I couldn't make a sound,
and now it's gone.
They might come down
this way again.
But then, I could be
wrong.

No Wool

Aching limbs
obliged
to sit,
our empty hands
receive
no wool to knit;
no wool.

No wonder,
as we sit and stare,
the ticking clock,
high on the wall,
concerns us
not at all.

Question

You look at me.
I look at you.
Is there nothing
we can
do?

SECTION III - NO EXIT

Second Wife

I can't think
what is it I've done;
my memory isn't clear.
He has a daughter and a son.
I've never seen them here.

He married for a second time
and I became his wife.
I love him so!
Where is he now?
We had a lovely life.

Here, I'm alone
and don't know why,
or who
I have become.
And if I could I'd run away
like others here have done.

Now I feel panic
every day;
some underlying fear.
Each hour is feeling
like a trap,
ten minutes like
a year.

Handbag

Are they in here,
the keys to my door?
What is it that I'm looking for?
A bit of biscuit, a piece of lace,
sweet wrappers all over the place.
Ah! Here's my purse –
the most important thing!
Oh, it's empty.
Where's my ring?
Who are these people?
I'm all alone,
sitting,
waiting
to go home.

My car's outside.
It's there I know!
Please tell me
that I'm free
to go.

Mayday Call

What to do? I'm lost,
at sea.
Please come in and rescue me.
There is no phone
for us to use.
Each one of us alone,
confused.
Mayday! Mayday!
Rescue me.
Somewhere alone
and all at sea.

Polite Request

Excuse me!
Please do understand
we only meant to stay a day
and now we'd like
to go away.

I think we came here
in my car.
We're leaving now,
we don't live far.

Please show us
where to pay the bill.
This place seems for
the very ill.

Departure

Plan A

I think
my husband's
coming today.
Let's ask him
to take us both away.

I think
my husband's
coming too.
Shall we go with him,
or shall I go with you?

Plan B

There's a bus stop nearby.
Are you ready to go?
We'll say, 'Thank you,
we're leaving.'

Do you want to stay?
No!

SECTION IV - HOW IT ALL BEGAN

Message

I think I rang you yesterday;
something I had to say.
I wanted you to tell me
if tomorrow was today.
I know you said you'd meet me
at the bottom of the street
and, as you said it yesterday,
is it today we meet?
I rang you up this morning
then remembered
you weren't well.
I hope you do recover soon
but you never can tell.
I waited on the corner
and then went home again.
I must have set out
several times and
stood there in the rain.
I'm leaving you this message.
Sorry to be a pain.
Perhaps,
when you receive it,
you could call me back again.

Secateurs

I'm looking for the secateurs.
The ones I gave to you?
Let's try and find them then.
How very nice of you!
You said you'd do the garden.
You put them by the door.
I got them from the garage.
You put them on the floor;
the ones with yellow handles
so you'll see them on the ground.
We'd better try and find them
if you think they can be found.
Have you tried your pocket
in the waistcoat which you wear
when you go into the garden
to take the morning air?
Are they the ones you gave me?
They are so light and good.
One birthday, I remember now,
the handles made of wood.
I'm going to the garden;
I'll get my secateurs.
I'm not sure how you spell it.
I think it's a French word.
I'll make a note to look it up.
I haven't time just now.
I must go in the garden.
I'll only be an hour.

I'll come in when I'm finished.
You go and have a rest.
You're looking rather tired now;
I know you've done your best.
I'll see you in a jiffy,
There's so much work to do.
It may pour down much later
so only now will do.
I've got my gloves and basket,
so I suggest you go.
We'll have a sherry afterwards
and then perhaps you'll mow.

Diagnosis Blues *

Trouble in kind
that's new!
Takes the key out
from my door.
I've got the D-Day blues.
Trouble in mind
for sure.

Somebody broke
the news.
Humped my boat up
on the shore.
Unlaced my shoes.
Things aren't so good
any more.

I hear a bell that chimes.
Got the D-Day news
today.
Looks like the blues have come;
have truly come
my way.

*A re-working of jazz composer Richard M Jones'
'Trouble in Mind', 1924*

Doctor's Review

Good morning!
How's the brain?
Better, worse
or just the same?

Forecast Unsettled

There is a word; it starts
dement ...
that you will never say.
It speaks of a predicament
that will not go away;
the forecast dull and
inclement
even though it's May.
And to your side
I have been sent
never to go away,
as if to you
I had been lent.

There is a word that starts
dement ... that
you will never hear.
How well you teach me
what is meant
as year passes each year.
And by your side
I represent
your tender soul
my dear,
as if to you
I had been lent
never to
disappear.

There is a place
where lives are spent
with madness in the air.
The forecast dull
and inclement.
No one
knows what
to wear.

Context

How sad it is
to reminisce
in the midst
of all of this.

The Connection
About the Author

Vanessa Young's working life took place in London. As a mother of two, she gradually changed career from secretarial employment to working in adult education. As this change took place, she obtained two hard-earned degrees and various professional teaching qualifications. For a considerable amount of this time, she was living within a community of The Society of Friends (Quakers) and it was then that she first entered a residential care home to visit an elderly friend.

She began developing and teaching courses in English as a Second or Community Language across three London boroughs as well as a wide range of English as a Foreign Language (EFL) courses at Goldsmiths University. While studying she often focused on older learners and looked into the University of The Third Age (U3A) as well as the concept of 4th Age learners stimulated by the work of Laslett and Midwinter. Inspired by their direction of travel, Young chose to move this continuing interest into the care home setting as a dissertation topic studying the formative years of what is now the National Activity Providers Association, NAPA, as well as devising and leading some Activities herself in a welcoming and well-run care home in Peckham, south-east London.

On retiring, and still in London, a leaflet through her door led Young to undertake a short introductory course in care work, which included uniformed work over three shift patterns in a large care home. This was on the brink of what turned out to be an as-yet-unknown thirteen-year period as primary carer for her mother who, as it happened, was in the second year of early-onset Alzheimer's but still living alone, at home in a Dorset village, and managing with an arranged hour or two's oversight per week. Young's experience to date had barely touched on dementia itself. Neither was it a word she and her mother had ever used together in conversation.

A crisis developed and Young set about wrapping up her London life to partner her mother in what was to be a prolonged and quite unpredictable continuing education in the world of the elderly care sector, starting right at the beginning, the last six or so years involving residential care.

It soon became apparent that the status of daughter/primary carer granted no opportunity to offer comment or to influence the increasingly trying situations they found themselves in. Young was therefore inadvertently recruited into an open-ended training of unaccustomed observation as stage moved to stage. The experience of exclusion from positive inclusivity in any policy or procedure became all the more pressing as the disease took hold, and respite turned into residency. When the inevitable end of life came it was fifteen years after diagnosis and Young's mother was six months shy of her one hundredth birthday.

So it was that *Precious Work* finally came about. It was after a lengthy gestation period that Vanessa Young resorted to one of her own personal pursuits, that of writing poetry and verse, to explain what she had witnessed, and to come up with her idea to use it educationally as a tool for those working, or in any way involved, in the profession of caring for men and women who turn up in the Specialist Dementia Units of care homes.

Acknowledgements

With gratitude to my son Dominic and my daughter Ciara.

Thanks to Ray Tracey who helped me care for my mother, Elisabeth Anne, and co-witnessed many of the situations described in these poems, to Norman Hartley who has believed in me from the outset, and all those who have supported me, including Lesley Benham MBE, Sheila McCaughey, Eric Midwinter OBE, Jean Seymour, Rita Upchurch MBE.

My thanks also to The Harbour Poets, in Weymouth, now led by Richard Green, and their founder the late Elsa Corbluth, for invaluable friendship and support.

I also owe a debt to The Society of Friends (Quakers).

And, lastly, thanks to Linda Dobbs for bringing this project to fruition.

Purpose

The goal of this unusual volume is that it should be an aid to promote the kind of discussion that stimulates the desire, imagination, understanding and ability to brighten and inform a radiating network of good practice, and to generate forces of change as a matter of course where stagnant malpractice has become an acceptable norm for whatever reason.

☙